Brigitte Casagranda

Napkin Découpage

Search Press

To Marie, Sophie and Baptiste.

*With grateful thanks to my parents
for their valuable help.*

Graphic design   cora.M

Cora Martineau • Laudonie • 24390 • Tourtoirac

First published in Great Britain 2004 by
Search Press Limited
Wellwood, North Farm Road, Tunbridge Wells, Kent
TN2 3DR

Originally published in France by
LTA, a department of Meta-Éditions
Original title: *Collages de serviettes en papier sur tous supports Volume 3*
© 2003, LTA, a department of Meta-Éditions
Dépôt légal : October 2003
Photography: Mariane Hufschmitt
Photo-engraving : Leyre

English translation by Norman Porter
English translation © Search Press Limited 2004

ISBN 1 84448 021 6

The publishers and author can accept no responsibility
for any consequences arising from the information,
advice or instructions given in this publication.

Contents

Introduction

MATERIALS

An amazing variety of beautiful decorative paper napkins are available. What a shame just to use them and then throw them away! The napkins featured in this book yield a wealth of motifs, patterns and borders that will give lasting pleasure to family and friends. They can be applied to many different surfaces and given as gifts, or you can decorate your own home with some of the projects on the following pages. The techniques are simple and clearly explained.

Don't worry if you can't find the napkin designs shown here, because you are sure to be able to find suitable substitutes. Just bear in mind when you are buying them that the sizes and shapes of the motifs must be appropriate to the sizes and shapes of your blanks and surfaces.

Other items
- Napkin glue
- Crackle glaze
- Scissors
- Acrylic paint
- Gouache varnish
- Wood varnish
- Acrylic varnish
- Varnish brush
- Sponges

BLANKS AND SURFACES

Blank objects suitable for decoration can be found in art and craft shops, garden centres, via mail order companies, or you may have items at home that would be perfect. Choose objects with plain surfaces and make sure they are clean and properly prepared before applying your découpage.

Wood
There are many wooden items that can be decorated: trugs, boxes, trays, frames, furniture, flowerpot containers, beads, bracelets and more.

Tip Motifs can be glued directly on to the surface or, alternatively, if you do not want a plain wooden background, one or two coats of acrylic paint can be lightly dabbed on with a damp sponge.

If you would like to create an antiqued appearance, use a crackle varnish, (see the milk churn on page 40 and the umbrella stand on page 42).

Card
Boxes made of natural card can be found in craft shops and are available in a variety of sizes and shapes: round, oval, hexagonal and more. They are perfect for decorating.

Tip Motifs will stand out more clearly if you paint a card surface first.

Earthenware

You will find a wide choice of pots, vases, flowerpot containers and window boxes at larger garden centres.

Glassware

Many attractive plain glass containers and ornaments are available in kitchenware shops, supermarkets, garden centres or charity shops. They are all worth a visit to find suitable objects.

Tip Carefully clean any glass surface you wish to decorate with white spirit to remove any traces of grease.

Paper

Drawing books, cards, writing paper, carrier bags, and more, can all be decorated.

Tip When decorating a card, once the pattern is glued on and dry, iron the back of the card – with your iron set to 'steam' – then place it under a heavy book so it will remain flat.

Straw mats

Straw table mats and coasters can take on a beautiful new look when decorated with napkin découpage.

Metal

Metal is very fashionable now and you will find a large selection in florists, garden centres, hardware and department stores. Choose a project and see how easy it is to make a plant pot, milk churn, jug or an umbrella stand into an original gift.

Plastic

Art and craft shops offer a wide range of plastic objects suitable for decoration.

Candles

Candles are available in many different shapes and sizes. A festive theme is ideal and decorated candles look good in any setting, or they make ideal gifts for family and friends.

Polystyrene

Craft shops stock a wide variety of polystyrene blanks: eggs, baubles, wreaths and more.

Tip Paint blanks with acrylic paint before applying the motifs.

TECHNIQUE FOR CUT-OUT MOTIFS

With the napkin in one hand, use scissors to cut out the chosen motif as close as possible to its outline.

Separate the top layer of tissue on which the motif is printed from the under layers. You can place a tiny spot of napkin glue on your object to help hold the motif in position. Then, using a soft paintbrush which has been dipped in napkin glue, spread the glue over the motif, working from the centre out to the edges without pulling the design out of shape. Carefully smooth away wrinkles or air bubbles with the brush until you are happy with the result.

Apply a second coat of napkin glue over the whole surface, gently smoothing the motif out repeatedly. Leave to dry.

TECHNIQUE FOR TEAR-OUT MOTIFS

Hold the napkin in one hand and gently tear round the outline of the motif in an irregular way through all thicknesses, leaving a 0.5cm (1/4in) margin around the design. Carefully remove the under layers of the napkin, retaining the motif on the top layer.

Position the motif on your object. You can place a tiny spot of napkin glue on the surface to help hold it in position. Dip a soft paintbrush in the napkin glue and apply the glue over the motif, always starting from the centre of the design and moving out towards its edges.

Smooth the motif out with the brush to remove any wrinkles or air bubbles.

If you are adding more motifs, follow the

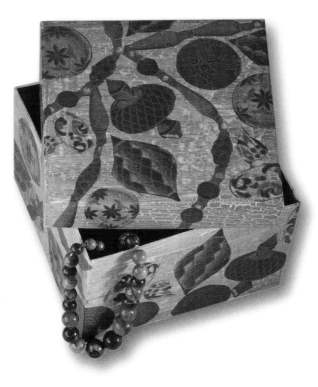

same process, and when they are all in position, apply a second layer of napkin glue over the whole object. Gently smooth out the motifs repeatedly. Leave to dry.

Tip When using a few motifs for complex, repetitive or geometric designs, lightly mark beforehand where they are going to be placed.

VARNISHING

Apply two or three coats of varnish to all surfaces made of wood, cork, cardboard or metal. You will have to wait twenty four hours between coats.

If you use a gouache varnish, two or three coats will be required, but as it is quick-drying you need only wait a few hours between applications.

Tip Brushes that are used for varnish or crackle glaze will need thorough cleaning. Read the manufacturers' instructions carefully.

Brushes that have been used to apply acrylic paint or napkin glue should be washed and thoroughly rinsed in clean, soapy water.

Autumn berries

CHEST OF DRAWERS
Autumn berry motifs

You will need
• Miniature chest
• Napkins with autumn berry motifs
• Paper scissors
• Nail scissors
• Napkin glue
• Soft paintbrush
• Wood varnish

Method
Carefully cut out the whole of the border motif. Use a pair of nail scissors to remove the background of the napkin, taking care not to damage any of the berries or leaves. Cut out the blackberry and acorn motifs printed in each corner of the napkin and follow the instructions on page 8.

Take a drop of napkin glue with the soft brush and, placing the motif in the centre of the first drawer, stick it down, brushing the glue from the centre of the motif towards the outer edges.

Repeat this motif at both corners of the drawer. Add a few red berries, filling in the spaces between the central motif and those glued in the corners.

Leave to dry.

Cut out more corner motifs, position them and glue them as shown on to the left and centre drawers in the middle row. For the right-hand drawer, choose another motif consisting of just red berries.

The two bottom drawers are also decorated with the corner motif. Position and glue this motif in the centre of the drawers.

You will be able to add a few leaves in each corner of the drawer, cut from the border frieze.

Decorate the sides of the chest using the border motif, filling in any spaces with red berries. Leave to dry.

Apply a coat of wood varnish to the whole chest. Leave to dry for twenty four hours then apply a second coat.

DISPLAY CASE
Autumn berry motifs

You will need
- **Glass-fronted display case**
- **Napkins decorated with a landscape**
- **Napkins with autumn berry motifs**
- **Scissors**
- **Napkin glue**
- **Soft paintbrush**
- **Wood varnish**

Method
Open the display case so that you can decorate the back of the case using three landscape napkins. Tear off the row of vines on the bottom of one napkin, using the tear-off technique described on page 8. Do this once more so that you end up with two rows of vines. These will be used as the foreground in the scene you are creating. Now tear out the whole landscape. Cut the edges with scissors.

Carefully arrange these three motifs, as shown below, so they overlap and glue them into position using a soft brush and napkin glue (see page 8). Take care that the three rows of vines are aligned vertically, giving the appearance of a hedge.

Allow to dry.

Decorate the interior and exterior of the case with berries cut out from the border of the autumn berries napkin. Make sure that the motifs will fit into the required length and width.

Only use red berries to decorate the top of the case. Leave to dry.

Apply two coats of wood varnish to the outside of the case, leaving twenty four hours between each application.

Once the varnish is dry you will be able to fix the case to the wall and it will be ready for your display.

The finished decorated case would provide an ideal setting for a collection of porcelain birds or animals.

BOX
Autumn berry motifs

You will need
- A wooden box
- Napkins with autumn berry motifs
- Scissors
- Napkin glue
- Soft paintbrush
- Wood varnish

Method

Cut out the border motif from an autumn berry napkin, following the instructions for the cut-out technique (see page 8), then carefully cut out the two blackberry and acorn corner motifs. These will be used to decorate the box lid.

Place a spot of napkin glue where you want to centre the first motif. Place it in position and using a soft brush dipped in napkin glue, work from the centre of the motif, and spread the glue towards the outer edges. Carefully apply the other corner motif in the same way. Leave to dry.

The exterior sides of the box are decorated with red berries. Cut them out of the border and glue them into position, using the same method as above. Leave to dry.

Apply two coats of wood varnish, leaving twenty four hours between applications.

FRAME
Autumn berries motifs

You will need
- A frame
- Napkins with autumn berry motifs
- Scissors
- Napkin glue
- Soft paintbrush
- Wood varnish

Method
Cut out the blackberry and acorn motif at the corner of the border. Position it in the bottom left hand corner of the frame and stick it in place with napkin glue using a soft paintbrush (see page 8). Cut out a few leaves and berries. Glue them in place to extend the decoration part way up the side and part way along the bottom.

Leave to dry.

Apply two coats of wood varnish, leaving twenty four hours between applications.

DISHES
Wreaths of apples and leaves with bows

You will need
- Three dishes
- Napkins with apples, leaves and bows
- Scissors
- Napkin glue
- Soft paintbrush

Method
The wreaths on the napkins can be used in various ways to decorate your dishes. Follow the instructions on page 8.

For the first dish, cut out a whole wreath motif but keep just the central part which contains the bow, that is to say a quarter of the wreath. Cut out three of these motifs end to end, to form a garland that loops round the outside of the dish.

For the second dish, you can reverse the garland design. Position a dish upside down

on your worktable and glue the motifs which are placed as garlands from the base towards the rim of the dish. Add bows, removing the ribbons, and fix them in the empty spaces with napkin glue.

Leave to dry.

For the third dish, cut a wreath into individual apples and leaves and use these evenly spaced around the rim. Leave to dry.

Apply a coat of napkin glue.

Leave to dry.

BOWLS

Wreaths of apples and leaves with bows

You will need
- **Small wooden bowls**
- **Napkins with apple, leaf and bow motifs**
- **Scissors**
- **Napkin glue**
- **Soft paintbrush**
- **Wood varnish**

Method

Carefully cut out a whole wreath of fruit and the bow. Centre it on a bowl and glue it in position using a paintbrush dipped in napkin glue (see page 8). Spread the glue out from the centre of the motif towards the inner edge and then towards the outer edge of the bowl to prevent the paper design being pulled out of shape.

Leave to dry.

You can vary the decoration by cutting up the wreath into three or four equal parts which you can then place around the rim of a bowl and glue end to end. Then arrange the bow motif with some fruit in the centre of the bowl and fix it with a little napkin glue. Leave to dry.

Apply two coats of wood varnish, leaving twenty four hours between applications.

Birds

TIT'S NESTBOX
Blue tit and great tit motifs

You will need
- Wooden nestbox
- Napkins with blue and great tit motifs
- Scissors
- Acrylic paint, grey and white
- Napkin glue
- Soft paintbrush
- Fine paintbrush
- Wood varnish

Method

Apply two coats of grey acrylic paint over the whole surface of the nestbox and leave to dry. Cut out the blue tits and great tits. Place and then glue, one by one, the blue tits and great tits on the sides and roof of the nestbox, following the instructions on page 8. Leave to dry.

With acrylic paint and a fine brush, paint snowflakes on the nestbox. Leave to dry.

Protect the box by applying three coats of wood varnish, leaving twenty four hours between applications.

ROBIN'S NESTBOX
Robin motifs

You will need
- Wooden nestbox
- Napkins with robin motifs
- Scissors
- Acrylic paint, Arctic blue and light blue
- Soft paintbrush
- Sponge
- Wood varnish

Method

Apply a coat of Arctic blue acrylic paint to the whole surface of the nestbox, then gently sponge light blue paint randomly on to the surface. Leave to dry.

Tear out the robin motifs as described in the tear-out technique on page 8. Place and stick them on to the sides and roof of the nestbox, applying the napkin glue to the centre of the motifs and spreading it out evenly towards the edges. Leave to dry.

Protect the box by applying three coats of wood varnish, leaving twenty four hours between applications.

Tip A book about birds will tell you the size and type of aperture required to attract nesting blue tits, great tits or robins and will also tell you about the best places to hang nesting boxes.

GIFT BAG
Blue tit and great tit motifs

You will need
- White paper carrier bag
- Napkins with great and blue tit motifs
- Scissors
- Soft paintbrush
- Napkin glue

Method
Cut out the entire central motif in one piece, including the string (see page 17). Cut out a few individual birds following the instructions on page 8. Position the seed ring in the centre of the bag and glue it in place with a soft paintbrush and napkin glue. Add extra birds around the circumference of the seed ring.

Leave to dry.

A variation on this idea would be to tear out a few small fir trees and glue them as a border around the bottom of the bag. Place them at regular intervals. Leave to dry.

FESTIVE CACHE-POT
Blue tit and great tit motifs

You will need
- Painted metal cache-pot
- Napkins with great and blue tit motifs
- Scissors
- Soft paintbrush
- Fine paintbrush
- Napkin glue
- Acrylic paint, white

Method
Cut out a few of the birds. Position and glue them, one by one, on the cache-pot, following the instructions on page 8.

Leave to dry.

Add snowflakes with a fine paintbrush and white acrylic paint. Leave to dry.

CHRISTMAS CACHE-POT
Robin motifs

You will need
- **A white painted metal cache-pot**
- **Napkins with robin motifs**
- **Napkin glue**
- **Soft paintbrush**

Method
Tear out a few robin motifs following the tear-out technique described on page 8.

Position them and stick them one by one to the cache-pot using napkin glue.

Leave to dry.

If you would like to use the pot again with a different design, do not varnish over the motifs, then they will be easy to remove after a soaking in hot water.

In this way the decoration can be changed according to the celebration or season.

Ivy wreaths and festive garlands

DOLL'S CRADLE
Garland motifs

You will need
- Wooden doll's cradle
- Napkin with heart garland motifs
- Acrylic paint, white
- Acrylic paint, pale yellow
- Scissors
- Napkin glue
- Soft paintbrush
- Wood varnish

Method
Apply a coat of white paint evenly over the cradle. Leave to dry. Apply a coat of pale yellow paint which has been diluted with a little white paint. The motifs will stand out more clearly against this painted background Leave to dry.

Cut out two heart-shaped garlands, following the instructions on page 8. Carefully glue them to the exterior surface of each cradle end.

Cut out pieces of the garland motif. Place the pieces end to end, and glue them to the side edges of the cradle and to the interior contours of the cradle head.

Leave to dry.

You could also add two red bows cut from a wreath.

Apply three coats of wood varnish to the cradle, leaving twenty four hours between applications. Leave to dry.

DOLL'S CHAIR
Garland motifs

You will need
- Wooden doll's chair
- Napkins with heart garland motifs
- Napkin glue
- Scissors
- Acrylic paint, white
- Acrylic paint, pale yellow
- Soft paintbrush
- Wood varnish

Method
Apply a coat of white paint evenly over the chair. Leave to dry.

Apply a coat of pale yellow paint which has been diluted with a little white paint.

Leave to dry.

Cut out a heart-shaped garland and centre it on the seat. Brush on napkin glue from the mid-line of the motif towards its inner, and then towards its outer edges following the instructions on page 8. Leave to dry.

Apply three coats of wood varnish to the chair, leaving twenty four hours between applications.

SPINNING TOP
Ivy wreath, fir cones and red bow motifs

You will need
- Wooden spinning top
- Acrylic paint, white
- Acrylic paint, pale yellow
- Napkin with ivy wreath motif
- Scissors
- Soft paintbrush
- Napkin glue
- Wood varnish

Method
Apply a coat of white paint evenly over the top. Leave to dry. Apply a coat of pale yellow paint which has been diluted with a little white paint. Leave to dry.

Cut out the ivy wreath, then cut round the inside perimeter of the wreath to remove the centre.

Centre the wreath on the top and glue it to the surface, following the instructions on page 8. Work the glue from the centre of the top towards the outer edges of the motif. Leave to dry.

Apply two coats of wood varnish to the top, leaving twenty four hours between applications.

HEART BOX
Ivy garland motif

You will need
- Wooden heart-shaped box
- Acrylic paint, white
- Acrylic paint, pale yellow
- Napkin with ivy garland motif
- Scissors
- Soft paintbrush
- Napkin glue
- Wood varnish

Method
Apply a coat of white paint evenly over the box. Leave to dry. Apply a coat of pale yellow paint which has been diluted with a little white paint. Leave to dry.

Cut out the heart-shaped wreath, place it on the lid of the box and brush on the napkin glue following the instructions on page 8. Leave to dry.

Apply two coats of wood varnish, leaving twenty four hours between applications.

ROUND BOX
Ivy wreath, fir cones and red bow motif with star motif

You will need
- **Round box**
- **Acrylic paint, white**
- **Acrylic paint, pale yellow**
- **Napkins with ivy wreath and star motif**
- **Scissors**
- **Soft paintbrush**
- **Napkin glue**
- **Wood varnish**

Method
Apply a coat of white paint evenly over the box. Leave to dry. Apply a coat of pale yellow paint which has been diluted with a little white paint. Leave to dry.

Cut out the ivy wreath. Cut out patches of foliage from the fir tree star design.

Place the ivy wreath on the lid of the box and brush on the napkin glue, working from the inner edge outwards and following the instructions on page 8.

Decorate the sides of the box with the patches of foliage, carefully applying them one by one. Leave to dry.

Apply two coats of wood varnish, leaving twenty four hours between applications.

PHOTOGRAPH ALBUM
Ivy garland and gold lettering motifs

You will need
- **Photograph album with wooden covers**
- **Napkin with ivy garland motif**
- **Scissors**
- **Napkin glue**
- **Soft paintbrush**
- **Wood varnish**

Method
Carefully cut out the lettering. Cut out the heart-shaped garland, then cut out the centre.

Position the heart in the centre of the front cover of the album and gently brush napkin glue over the surface, following the instructions on page 8.

Add the lettering around the wreath, mixing up the various phrases.

Leave to dry.

Apply two coats of wood varnish leaving twenty four hours between applications.

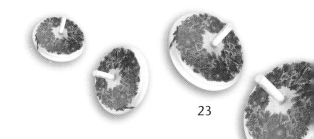

Christmas

LARGE CANDLE
Christmas stocking motifs

You will need
- Candle 23cm (9in) tall
- Napkins with Christmas stocking motifs
- Scissors
- Soft paintbrush
- Candle varnish

Method

Carefully cut out the stocking motifs. You will need at least nine of these if you want to spiral them around the candle. You can use a pin to help you calculate the position and the space between each of the motifs.

Place a stocking motif on the candle. Using the soft paintbrush, gently apply the candle varnish over the surface, following the instructions on page 8. Apply more motifs in the same way. Leave to dry.

Apply a coat of candle varnish over the whole surface of the candle. Leave to dry.

Tip Never leave a candle unattended.

FESTIVE CANDLE
Christmas tree motifs

You will need
- A candle 13 cm (5in) tall
- Napkins with Christmas tree motifs
- Scissors
- Soft paintbrush
- Candle varnish

Method

Cut out the Christmas trees with the toy motifs, then cut out a purple border. Place the border around the base of the candle and brush on a little candle varnish, following the instructions on page 8. Leave to dry.

Wrap the Christmas trees round the candle and brush on the candle varnish from the centre of the motif to the edges, taking care not to pull the designs out of shape. Leave to dry.

Apply a coat of candle varnish over the whole surface of the candle. Leave to dry.

SMALL CANDLE
Toy frieze motif

You will need
- A white candle 8cm (3¼ in) tall
- Napkins with toy motifs
- Scissors
- Soft paintbrush
- Candle varnish

Method
Cut out the toy frieze in its entirety. Also cut out the purple border and, using the soft brush and candle varnish, secure this around the candle base, following the instructions on page 8.

Place the toy frieze just above the purple border and secure it to the candle in the same way. Spread the varnish gently from the centre of the motif outwards.

Leave to dry.

Apply a coat of candle varnish over the whole surface of the candle. Leave to dry.

Tip Never leave a candle unattended.

CANDLE CONTAINERS
Toy and border motifs

You will need
- Three glass candle containers
- Napkins with toy and border motifs
- Scissors
- Soft paintbrush
- Napkin glue

Method
Cut out a single width purple border and a double width purple border. Cut out the toy frieze, excluding the Christmas tree.

Secure the single width border round the top edge of the container using a paintbrush and napkin glue, following the instructions on page 8. Leave to dry.

Apply the double width purple border around the bottom of the container, then the toy frieze in between the borders using the same method. Leave to dry.

Apply a coat of napkin glue over the whole surface. Leave to dry.

STRAW TABLE MATS
Stockings, toy frieze and Christmas tree motifs

You will need
- Straw table mats
- Napkins with Christmas tree, stocking and toy frieze motifs
- Scissors
- Glue-varnish
- Soft paintbrush

Method
These napkins can be used to create a set of seasonal mats with as many different designs as your imagination allows.

Cut out the borders, stockings, toy frieze and Christmas trees.

On one mat you could have a stocking motif in the centre with the purple border surround. Similarly, you could use a section of toy frieze as the centre of another mat and, on another, a Christmas tree. Play around with the designs. They can be combined, or used with borders or without. No two need be alike.

Remember, when applying larger motifs: begin by applying glue at the centre and spread it out gently towards the motif's outer edges, following the instructions on page 8.

GLASS DISHES FOR CANDLES
Toy frieze and border motifs

You will need
- Three glass candle dishes
- Napkins with border and toy motifs
- Scissors
- Napkin glue
- Soft paintbrush

Method
Cut out the single width purple border, double width border and the toy frieze, including the Christmas tree.

Turn the dishes upside down.

Glue the single width border round one of the dishes, following the instructions on page 8.

Leave to dry.

Glue the double width border around another dish following the same method.

Leave to dry.

Cut out a section of the toys frieze and glue it to the bottom of the third dish following the same method.

Leave to dry.

Apply two coats of napkin glue to all the dishes, leaving twenty four hours between applications.

GIFT SACHETS
Christmas bauble motifs

You will need
- Two white gift sachets
- Napkins with Christmas motifs
- Scissors
- Napkin glue
- Soft paintbrush

Method
Cut out the Christmas bauble motifs.

Glue them on to one side of each sachet, spreading the glue evenly from the centre of the motifs outwards, following the instructions on page 8.

Leave to dry.

FESTIVE BAG
Christmas tree motifs

You will need
- White carrier bag
- Napkins with Christmas tree motifs
- Scissors
- Nail scissors
- Napkin glue
- Soft paintbrush

Method
Cut out the Christmas tree motifs and arrange them carefully on the front of the carrier bag, then glue them in position following the instructions on page 8.

Cut out several garlands using the nail scissors and glue these over selected

garlands between the Christmas baubles to slightly raise the design. Leave to dry.

Apply napkin glue over the whole design. Leave to dry.

CHRISTMAS BAUBLES
Father Christmas motifs

You will need
• Clear plastic balls and ovals that can be opened into halves, medallions and fir trees
• Napkins with Father Christmas motifs
• Scissors
• Acrylic paint, white
• Napkin glue
• Soft paintbrush

Method
Cut out the Father Christmas heads.

Open the balls. Holding a half sphere in your palm, centre a motif, right side down, on the surface. Holding it in place with your index finger, take some napkin glue and apply it to the centre of the motif with the brush, spreading the glue out to the edges. Be careful to avoid tearing or pulling the motif out of shape and follow the instructions on page 8.

Leave to dry then cut off any excess paper.

Apply a coat of white paint to the interior of the half sphere so that the motif shows up really well. Leave to dry.

Repeat this process on all of the half spheres, then apply this technique to all the other shapes.

KEY RINGS

Father Christmas, dove and poinsettia motifs

You will need
- Key rings with flat wooden fobs
- Napkins with Father Christmas, dove and poinsettia motifs
- Scissors
- Napkin glue
- Acrylic paint, white
- Acrylic varnish
- Soft paintbrush

Method
Cut out a selection of motifs the same size as the key fobs.

Apply a coat of white acrylic paint to the fob surfaces. Glue the motifs to the fobs, following the instructions on page 8. Leave to dry.

Apply two coats of varnish, allowing each coat to dry before applying the next.

FATHER CHRISTMAS CANDLE

Father Christmas motifs

You will need
- Candle 12 cm (4 3/4 in) tall
- Napkins with Father Christmas motifs
- Scissors
- Candle varnish
- Soft paintbrush

Method

Cut out two Father Christmas motifs.

Place one Father Christmas on the candle and, working from the centre of the motif outwards, apply candle varnish using the paintbrush, following the instructions on page 8.

Apply the second Father Christmas to the other side of the candle.

Leave to dry.

Tip Never leave a candle unattended.

CHRISTMAS CANDLE WREATH
Father Christmas motifs

You will need
• Polystyrene wreath base
• Napkins with Father Christmas and dove motifs
• Napkin glue
• Scissors
• Soft paintbrush

Method

Cut out Father Christmas heads as well as sections of sky and a few doves.

Cover the entire surface of the wreath base, applying the motifs one at a time so that they overlap slightly, following the instructions on page 8. Leave to dry.

Cut out the green frieze and apply it in bands at regular intervals around the wreath.

Leave to dry.

Apply a coat of napkin glue. Leave to dry.

Geese and ribbons

WOODEN CLOGS
Ribbon and holly frieze motifs

You will need
- Two pairs of wooden clogs: one for an adult, one for a child
- Napkins with goose and ribbon motifs
- Scissors
- Napkin glue
- Soft paintbrush
- Wood varnish

Method for the adult's clogs
Cut out six bows with scissors and tear out a double thickness border with your fingers, following the instructions on page 8. Keep the border double thickness for the edge of the foot entrance, as it needs to be harder wearing here. Also tear out lots of small patches of holly from the frieze.

Glue part of the border round the rim smoothing it out as you work the glue into the surface.

Apply another section of border across the arch of the foot. Place a bow in the centre of the clog, glue it and then add two more bows on either side of it.

Using the same method, add small pieces of holly on the toe of the clog.

Leave to dry.

Repeat on the other clog.

Apply two coats of wood varnish to the clogs, leaving twenty four hours between each application.

Method for the child's clogs
Tear out the border for the rim of the foot entrance, as for the adult clogs. Glue it in position, following the instructions on page 8. Leave to dry.

Place and glue a bow on the outer side of the clog so that the ribbons trail across the front. Glue down small pieces of sky and snowflakes in the empty spaces.

Apply two coats of wood varnish, leaving twenty four hours between applications.

WATERING CAN
Goose with ribbon motifs

You will need
- A metal watering can
- Napkins with goose and ribbon motifs
- Scissors
- Napkin glue
- Soft paintbrush
- Acrylic paint, white
- Acrylic paint, light blue
- Sponge
- Acrylic varnish
- Fine paintbrush

Method
Sponge white paint over the whole surface of the watering can. Leave to dry.

Cut out several geese. Using your fingers, tear out enough patches of sky to cover the watering can. Tear off a single holly border and then a double thickness holly border.

Glue the geese round the can, following the instructions on page 8. Next, glue sky pieces edge to edge round the geese, then over the whole surface of the watering can, just leaving the handle.

Leave to dry.

Glue a border of holly around the top rim and round the base of the watering can.

Apply the double thickness holly border along and underneath the handle, pressing it in well so that it adopts the handle's form.

Leave to dry.

With a fine brush and light blue acrylic paint, redefine the rim and bottom edge of the watering can.

Leave to dry.

Apply two coats of acrylic varnish to the watering can, allowing twenty four hours between each application.

FESTIVE CONTAINER
Ribbon and holly border motifs

You will need
- A small metal container
- Acrylic paint, white
- Napkins with goose and ribbon motifs
- Scissors
- Napkin glue
- Soft paintbrush
- Sponge
- Acrylic varnish

Method
This container would be ideal for a plant arrangement at Christmas either for your home or as a gift.

The first step is to sponge a coat of white acrylic paint over the exterior surface of the container. The motifs will not stand out as well if they are applied to unpainted metal.

Leave to dry.

Cut out sufficient ribbon motifs and tear out numerous strips of single and double bands of holly.

Glue a double border round the top rim of the container, smoothing it to shape with your finger and following the instructions on page 8. Glue a single band round the foot of the container.

Leave to dry.

Glue a bow to the front of the container, then frame it with a band of holly on each side. Continue in this way around the container.

Leave to dry.

Finally apply three coats of acrylic varnish, leaving twenty four hours between each application.

EARTHENWARE POT
Goose with ribbon motifs

You will need
- Earthenware pot
- Napkins with goose and ribbon motifs
- Scissors
- Card for stencil template
- Acrylic paint, white
- Napkin glue
- Soft paintbrush
- Crayon
- Acrylic varnish

Method
Cut out the number of geese you require for your pot, removing their legs.

To ensure the motif stands out against the earthenware, a stencil technique is used. Place a goose motif on the card, draw round it with the crayon, then cut away the shape of the goose.

Place this stencil on the pot and gently sponge white acrylic paint on to the surface through the goose shape.

Leave to dry.

Repeat this stencilling process twice more, at regular intervals around the pot.

Leave to dry.

Following the instructions on page 8, glue the goose motifs, one by one, over the white shapes. Smooth the surface to ensure that each one is without wrinkles or bubbles, before going on to glue down the next one.

Carefully add a few torn patches of sky around each goose.

Leave to dry.

Apply three coats of varnish, allowing each coat to dry for twenty four hours between applications.

Tip If you prefer a matt look, after you have finished decorating your pot, do not varnish it.

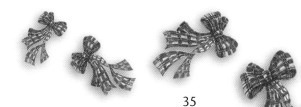

Hyacinths and snowdrops

JUG
Snowdrop motifs

You will need
• A white enamel jug
• Napkins with snowdrop motifs
• Scissors
• Nail scissors
• Napkin glue
• Soft paintbrush
•Acrylic varnish

Method
Carefully cut out lots of snowdrops. Use nail scissors to remove as much of the starry background as you can.

This design calls for a three deep frieze of snowdrops around the jug, each one slightly overlapped and offset to create the effect of a diagonal line.

Dab a little napkin glue on the jug where you want to centre the lower group of snowdrops. Place them close together with stems and flowers appearing to intertwine. Apply glue to the motifs, following the instructions on page 8. Leave a little drying time after finishing each one and gently smooth away any wrinkles or bubbles as you work. Leave to dry.

Apply a coat of acrylic varnish over the whole jug. Leave to dry.

TABLE
Snowdrop and hyacinth motifs

You will need
- Small wooden table
- Napkins with snowdrop motifs
- Napkins with hyacinth motifs
- Scissors
- Acrylic paint, white
- Soft paintbrush
- Napkin glue
- Wood varnish

Method
Apply a coat of white acrylic paint over the whole surface of the table. Leave to dry.

Cut out a number of snowdrop and hyacinth motifs.

First plan your design: place the motifs on the table surface and decide how you want them positioned.

Put a little napkin glue on your brush and glue the motifs down, following the instructions on page 8.

Place snowdrops close together, or even slightly overlapping. Allow one motif to dry a little before applying the next one. Take care not to damage the fragile stems or leaves.

Leave to dry before adding the hyacinths, following the same method.

Leave to dry.

Decorate legs and any other visible surfaces in the same way.

Apply two coats of wood varnish, leaving at least twenty four hours between each application.

VASE
Hyacinth motifs

You will need
- White vase
- Napkins with hyacinth motifs

- Scissors
- Napkin glue
- Soft paintbrush

Method

Cut out a number of hyacinth motifs.

Place a motif on the vase and hold it firmly. Dip the paintbrush in the napkin glue and place it in the centre of the motif, then carefully spread the glue from the centre of the hyacinth outwards, following the instructions on page 8. Slightly overlap the motifs, allowing each one to dry a little before applying the next. When the design is complete, leave it to dry.

Tip The design can be easily removed by soaking it in water. If you want to make the design more permanent, apply one final coat of napkin glue. Leave to dry.

STORAGE JAR
Hyacinth motif

You will need
- Glass jar
- Napkins with hyacinth motifs
- Scissors
- Napkin glue
- Soft paintbrush

Method

Cut out only blue hyacinths, following the instructions on page 8. Work out first how many hyacinths you will need to create an evenly spaced design around the jar.

Place a tiny spot of glue on the glass surface, where you want to centre the first motif. Secure the hyacinth to the surface, spreading glue from the centre outwards.

Place and glue the rest of the motifs in the same way. Leave to dry.

Tip You can use a damp cotton bud to remove excess glue.

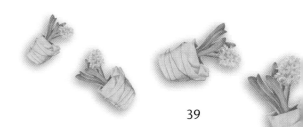

Poinsettias

MILK CHURN
Poinsettia motifs

You will need
- **A metal milk can**
- **Napkins with poinsettia motifs**
- **Scissors**
- **Napkin glue**
- **Crackle varnish**
- **Acrylic paint, black**
- **Acrylic paint, ochre**
- **Soft paintbrush**
- **Hair dryer**
- **Acrylic varnish**

Method
Apply a coat of ochre acrylic paint to the surface of the milk churn. Leave to dry.

Apply a second coat of ochre. Leave to dry.

Apply a coat of crackle varnish, wait for twenty minutes, then apply a coat of black acrylic paint.

Now dry the surface with a hair dryer and the crackle effect will quickly appear.

Cut out several whole poinsettias.

Cut out some of the largest petals from several of them to create a number of smaller flowers.

Using the soft paintbrush and napkin glue, carefully apply the flowers, one by one, all over the can, following the instructions on page 8. Mix the large and small flowers together.

Leave to dry.

Apply two coats of varnish leaving three hours between applications.

UMBRELLA STAND
Poinsettia motifs

You will need
- Metal umbrella stand
- Napkins with poinsettia motifs
- Scissors
- Napkin glue
- Crackle varnish
- Acrylic paint, black and ochre
- Soft paintbrush
- Fine paintbrush
- Hair dryer
- Acrylic varnish

Method
Apply a coat of black acrylic paint to the whole surface of the umbrella stand. Leave to dry. Apply a coat of black paint. Leave to dry. Apply a coat of crackle varnish to the painted surface, wait for twenty minutes, then apply a coat of ochre acrylic paint over the top. Now dry the surface with a hair dryer and the crackle effect will quickly appear. Leave to dry.

Cut out several whole poinsettias. Cut out some of the largest petals from several of them to create a number of smaller flowers.

Position and glue the large poinsettias on to the surface of the umbrella stand, then the smaller ones between them, following the instructions on page 8. Leave to dry.

With a fine paintbrush, use some of the black acrylic paint to redefine the rolled rim of the umbrella stand. Leave to dry.

Apply two coats of acrylic varnish over the whole surface, leaving twenty four hours between applications.

CACHE-POT
Poinsettia motifs

You will need
- A metal cache-pot
- Napkins with poinsettia motifs
- Scissors
- Napkin glue
- Soft paintbrush
- Acrylic paint, black and ochre
- Crackle varnish
- Hair dryer
- Acrylic varnish

Method
Apply a coat of black acrylic paint evenly over the exterior of the cache-pot. Leave to dry.

Apply a second coat of black acrylic paint. Leave to dry.

Carefully brush a coat of crackle varnish over the painted surface and wait for twenty minutes. Apply a coat of ochre acrylic paint over the crackle glaze. Now dry the surface with a hair dryer and the crackle effect will quickly appear. Leave to dry.

Glue a large poinsettia motif in the centre of the cache pot, following the instructions on page 8. Surround it with smaller flowers made by removing the largest petals.

Smooth the motifs with a finger as you work, to prevent wrinkles and air bubbles forming. Leave to dry.

Carefully redefine the rolled metal edge of the container using black acrylic paint and a fine brush. Leave to dry.

Apply two coats of acrylic varnish, leaving three hours between applications.

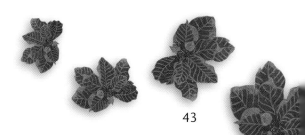

Polar bears

POLAR BEAR BOX
Polar bear motifs

You will need
- Card box 18 x 18cm (7 x 7in)
- Napkins with polar bear motifs
- Scissors
- Napkin glue
- Soft paintbrush
- Acrylic paint, white
- Acrylic paint, Arctic blue
- Crackle varnish
- Hair dryer
- Acrylic varnish

Method
Apply a coat of white acrylic paint to the box and lid. Leave to dry.

Cut out the polar bear, leaving enough background to fit the lid.

Carefully cut out four baby polar bears and four fir trees.

Apply a coat of crackle varnish to the sides of the lid and the sides of the box. Wait twenty minutes, then apply a coat of blue acrylic paint on top. Now dry the surface with a hair dryer and the crackle effect will quickly appear. Leave to dry.

Using napkin glue and a soft paintbrush, gently glue the large bear and background to the lid, following the instructions on page 8.

Leave to dry.

Decorate the sides of the box, alternating between the bear cubs and the fir trees. Leave to dry.

Apply two coats of acrylic varnish, leaving a few hours between applications.

FESTIVE BOX
Polar bear motifs

You will need
- **Card box 15 x 15cm (6 x 6in)**
- **Napkins with polar bear motifs**
- **Scissors**
- **Napkin glue**
- **Soft paintbrush**
- **Acrylic paint, white**
- **Acrylic paint, light blue**
- **Crackle varnish**
- **Hair dryer**
- **Acrylic varnish**

Method
Apply a coat of white acrylic paint to the box and lid. Leave to dry.

Work out how many polar bears will fit the lid and cut them out to fit.

Apply a coat of crackle varnish to the sides of the lid and the box. Wait twenty minutes and apply a coat of blue acrylic paint over the crackle varnish. Now dry the surface with a hair dryer and the crackle effect will quickly appear.

Position a polar bear, or bears, on the lid and glue them to the surface, following the instructions on page 8. Working from the centre outwards, smooth away any wrinkles or air bubbles.

Leave to dry.

Apply two coats of varnish to the box allowing a few hours drying time between applications.

OVAL POLAR BEAR CUB BOX

Polar bear cub motifs

You will need

- Oval card box 8 cm (3 1/4 in) diameter
- Napkins with bear cub motifs
- Scissors
- Napkin glue
- Soft paintbrush
- Fine paintbrush
- Acrylic paint, white and blue
- Hair dryer
- Acrylic varnish

Method

Apply a coat of white acrylic paint to the lid and the sides of the box.

Leave to dry.

Apply a coat of crackle varnish to the box and lid. Wait twenty minutes, then apply a coat of blue acrylic paint on top. Now dry the surface with a hair dryer and the crackle effect will quickly appear. Leave to dry.

Place the bear cub on the centre of the lid and glue it down with napkin glue, following the instructions on page 8, and working from the centre outwards. Smooth away any wrinkles or air bubbles with your finger. Leave to dry.

Add a few snowflakes using white acrylic paint and the tip of a fine brush.

Leave to dry.

Finally, brush on two coats of acrylic varnish, leaving three hours between each application.

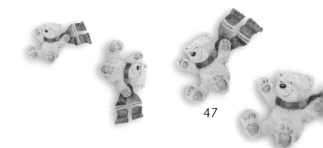

GIFT BAG
Polar bear motif

You will need
- A white carrier bag
- Napkin with polar bear motif
- Napkin glue
- Soft paintbrush

Method
Tear out the whole motif and some sky patches with your fingers following the instructions on page 8. Place the polar bear on the centre front of the bag.

Dip the brush in napkin glue and spread it over the motif and slightly over its edges, smoothing away any wrinkles or bubbles. Work slowly to avoid tearing the motif. Apply just touches of glue working from the centre of the motif outwards. Add the sky patches, and apply a coat of glue over the whole design.

POLAR BEAR CANDLE
Polar bear motif

You will need
- White candle 12 cm (4 3/4 in) tall
- Napkins with polar bear motifs
- Scissors
- Candle varnish
- Soft paintbrush

Method
Cut out a polar bear to fit the size of the candle.

Hold the motif firmly against the side of the candle and place a spot of candle varnish in the centre, then spread it outwards, following the instructions on page 8. Use small touches of glue to avoid distorting the motif. Gently smooth away any wrinkles or bubbles with a finger as you work. Leave to dry.

Tip Never leave a candle unattended.

BEAR CUB CANDLE
Bear cub motifs

You will need
- White candle 8cm (3¼ in) tall
- Napkins with bear cub motifs
- Scissors
- Candle varnish
- Soft paintbrush

Method
Work out how many bear cubs will fit round the candle, then cut them out, including their scarves, following the instructions on page 8.

Place the cubs, one by one, around the candle, spacing them out regularly. As you place them, hold them firmly in position and brush candle varnish over them to secure them to the surface.

Leave to dry.

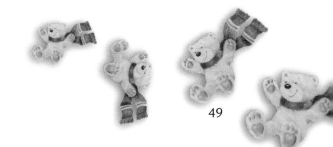

Bows

FESTIVE CANDLES
Green bow motifs

You will need
- Large candle 16 cm (6 ³/₄ in) tall
- Candle 13 cm (5in) tall
- Napkins with green bow motifs
- Scissors
- Candle varnish
- Soft paintbrush

Method
Carefully cut out four bows. Trim the ribbon ends neatly. These will be placed at the top and bottom of the candles.

Place one bow on a candle and smooth it on to the wax surface using the paintbrush dipped in candle varnish, following the instructions on page 8. Then apply the ribbon on the back of the candle.

Repeat on the other candle.

Leave to dry.

Tip Never leave a candle unattended.

STRAW CACHE-POT
Green bow motifs

You will need
- Straw cache-pot 18cm (7in) diameter
- Straw cache-pot 13cm (5in) diameter
- Napkins with green bow motifs
- Scissors
- Napkin glue
- Soft paintbrush

Method
You can apply napkin motifs to textured materials like woven straw successfully, but extra care is needed when applying the delicate tissue to slightly uneven surfaces.

First, cut out four bows and ribbons, following the instructions on page 8.

Apply one motif to the front of the cache-pot using the brush and napkin glue, gently smoothing it on to the surface. The ribbon ends should disappear over the rim and under the bottom edge. Repeat on the other side, and then on the other cache-pot.

WHITE POT
Green bow motifs

You will need
- White glazed earthenware pot
- Napkins with green bow motifs
- Scissors
- Napkin glue
- Soft paintbrush

Method
Carefully cut out the bow following the instructions on page 8.

Apply the bow to the front of the pot with napkin glue. Extend the ribbons to the rim and bottom edge, and around the middle of the pot. Work from the centre of the bow outwards, taking care not to tear or to pull the design out of shape.

Amaryllis

TABLE MATS
Amaryllis motifs

You will need
- **Straw table mats**
- **Napkins with amaryllis motifs**
- **Scissors**
- **Napkin glue**
- **Soft paintbrush**

Method
Tear round the flowers, then carefully cut round the pots, following the instructions on page 8.

Spread the motifs round the edge of the mats to help you calculate how many you will need and how much space there will be between each flower.

Dip the brush in the napkin glue, and apply the motifs to the mats one by one. Brush from the centre of each motif outwards, gently working the flowers into the textured surface.

Leave to dry.

DECORATIVE STRAW PLATE
Amaryllis motifs

You will need
- **Large straw plate**
- **Napkins with amaryllis motifs**
- **Scissors**
- **Napkin glue**
- **Soft paintbrush**

Method
For the rim of the plate, tear out lots of flower motifs retaining some of the gold background, and carefully cut out the pots, following the instructions on page 8.

Arrange flowers at equal distances round the rim and glue them in position with the brush and napkin glue, gently working the images into the textured surface.

Leave to dry.

Cut out enough border and apply it around the inside rim (see photograph opposite).

To decorate the centre of the plate, tear out lots of flowers with stalks, but without the pots. Position them closely side by side with the stalks pointing towards the centre of the plate. With a little napkin glue on the end of the brush, apply the flowers, one by one.

Complete the design with a single flower in the centre. Leave to dry.

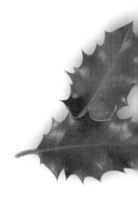

CAKE STAND
Amaryllis motifs

You will need
- **Glass cake stand**
- **Napkins with amaryllis motifs**
- **Scissors**
- **Napkin glue**
- **Soft paintbrush**

Method
Cut out several flowers with their pots, following the instructions on page 8.

Turn the cake stand upside down and position the motifs on the plate to work out how many you will need.

Dip the brush in napkin glue and apply the flowers to the underside of the plate one by one, working outwards from the centre of the motifs. Use a damp cotton bud to remove any excess glue.

Leave to dry.

Apply two coats of napkin glue, leaving twenty four hours between applications.

BOWL
Amaryllis motif

You will need
- White bowl
- Napkins with amaryllis motifs
- Scissors
- Napkin glue
- Soft paintbrush

Method
Carefully tear out a number of flowers with backgrounds. Use scissors to cut round the pots, following the instructions on page 8.

Place the motifs at regular intervals round the bowl then apply them one by one to the surface, starting with a drop of glue in the centre of a motif and spreading it outwards. Remove any excess glue with a damp cotton bud.

Leave to dry.

Apply two coats of napkin glue, leaving twenty four hours between applications.

FLOWER BOWL
Amaryllis motifs

You will need
- White bowl
- Napkins with amaryllis motifs
- Scissors
- Napkin glue

Method
Select two flowers in their pots. Carefully cut them out. Remove the stalks and stems and then cut out and retain the pots.

Following the instructions on page 8, apply the pots to the bowl, then the flowers, close to the pots. Remove traces of excess glue with a damp cotton bud. Leave to dry.

DECORATIVE STRAW COASTERS
Amaryllis motifs

You will need
- Straw coasters
- Napkins with amaryllis motifs
- Scissors

- **Napkin glue**
- **Soft paintbrush**

Method

Follow the instructions on page 8 and vary the designs. Tear out a large flower in its pot, with some of its golden background, then apply it in the centre of one coaster.

On another coaster add a border and place it along the top and bottom edges.

On the third coaster, tear out two smaller amaryllis plants keeping some of the gold background, and cut out the pots. Apply them to the centre of the coaster, leaving space between them.

Alternatively, individual flower heads could be cut out and used in different patterns, or bands of the border design could be overlaid with flowers.

Harlequins

GIFT BAG
Christmas tree decoration motifs

You will need
- **White paper gift bag**
- **Napkins with tree decoration motifs**
- **Scissors**
- **Napkin glue**
- **Soft paintbrush**

Method
Cut out the decorations.

Apply the decorations randomly over the back and front of the bag, following the instructions on page 8.

When applying the motifs, always work from the centre out, smoothing the surfaces with your finger to avoid any wrinkles or air bubbles.

Leave to dry. Apply a coat of napkin glue all over the design. Leave to dry.

NECKLACE
Christmas bauble motifs

You will need
- **Wooden beads**
- **Napkins with Christmas bauble motifs**
- **Scissors**
- **Napkin varnish**
- **Soft paintbrush**
- **Wooden sticks and a glass**
- **Acrylic varnish**

Method
Cut out the baubles and tear them into little pieces, following the instructions on page 8. Glue these, a piece at a time, on to the beads, overlapping them and keeping to the same colour for each one.

Place the wooden sticks in a glass, and then place the beads on the sticks. This will also make them easier to varnish. Leave to dry.

Apply two coats of acrylic varnish to the beads, leaving three hours between each application.

Thread the beads on to cord, alternating them with plain ones.

BRACELETS
Christmas bauble motifs

You will need
- Wooden bracelets
- Napkins with Christmas bauble motifs
- Scissors
- Napkin glue
- Acrylic varnish
- Soft paintbrush

Method
Cut out lots of bauble motifs and tear them into tiny pieces, following the instructions on page 8.

Decorate the interior and exterior surfaces of each bracelet. Work in stages and choose complementary colours to create bright, colourful designs. First apply pieces to the exterior surfaces, overlapping them slightly.

Leave to dry.

Apply pieces to the interior surfaces.

Leave to dry.

Apply two coats of acrylic varnish, leaving three hours between each application.

DECORATIVE BOX
Christmas bauble motif

You will need
- **Cube-shaped card box**
  15 x 15 x 15cm (6 x 6 x 6in)
- **Napkins with Christmas bauble motifs**
- **Scissors**
- **Acrylic paint, white and ochre**
- **Crackle varnish**
- **Acrylic varnish**
- **Soft paintbrush**
- **Hair dryer**

Method
Paint the whole box and lid with a coat of white acrylic paint. Leave to dry.

Apply a coat of crackle varnish. Leave to dry for twenty minutes.

Apply a coat of ochre acrylic paint. Now dry the painted surface with a hair dryer and the crackle effect will quickly appear.

Cut out lots of Christmas baubles, following the instructions on page 8. Also, carefully cut out the delicate garland motif.

Apply the baubles and garland motifs, one by one, to the box, randomly positioning the different shapes and colours. When you are applying the garland take care not to tear the fragile motif.

Decorate the lid in the same way.

Leave to dry.

Apply two coats of acrylic varnish over all the surfaces leaving three hours between each application.